THIS D-I-Y DIARY BELONGS TO:

_____
[name]

THIS DIARY WAS BEGUN ON: _____
[date]

If you are reading this book without my permission, beware! Your eyebrows will grow at the rate of .5 inches for every minute of reading. If you keep reading, an hour from now, your eyebrows will be 30 inches long. Consider yourself warned!

UNCLE JOHN'S D-I-Y DIARY: FOR INFOMANIACS ONLY

Portable Press is an imprint of the Printers Row Publishing Group, a Division of Readerlink Distribution Services, LLC. "Bathroom Reader," "Portable Press," and "Bathroom Readers' Institute" are registered trademarks of Readerlink Distribution Services, LLC. All rights reserved.

For information, write: The Bathroom Readers' Institute, P.O. Box 1117, Ashland, OR 97520
www.bathroomreader.com / e-mail: mail@bathroomreader.com

❦ Cover design by Jen Keenan ❦

❦ Cover and interior illustration by Nick Halliday ❦

The Bathroom Readers' Institute would like to thank the following people whose advice and assistance made this book possible:

Gordon Javna	Carly Schuna	Sydney Stanley
Kim T. Griswell	Hannah L. Bingham	Blake Mitchum
Trina Janssen	Melinda Allman	Rusty von Dyl
Brian Boone	Jennifer Magee	Aaron Guzman
Jay Newman	Peter Norton	Iggie the Chameleon

ISBN-13: 978-1-62686-462-7 ❦ ISBN 10: 1-62686-462-4

Printed in the United States of America

First Printing

19 18 17 16 15 1 2 3 4 5

Uncle John's
D-i-Y DiARY

FOR iNFOMANiACS ONLY!

By Marti Fartiamo
and You!

THE BATHROOM READERS' iNSTiTUTE
ASHLAND, OREGON

*InfoBit: An <u>infoManiac</u> is someone who craves facts the way most people crave ice cream.

PS: It's okay to crave ice cream, too.

PPS: By the way, did you know that the first ice cream cone was served at the 1904 St. Louis World's Fair?

WONDERING WHY I'M HIDING IN THIS TREE? SEE PAGE 155.

Marti's Guide to Information Domination

HERE'S A FACT: Research says that until about age 12, girls are smarter than boys. (Sorry, guys...with any luck, you'll catch up.) Scientists say girls are smarter because they mature faster than boys. I don't know about other girls, but I'm not smart because I'm more mature (although...I definitely am). I'm smart because I keep growing my brain.

How? Simple! The brain is a muscle. Just like any other muscle it grows through EXERCISE. The best way I know to exercise my brain is to LEARN SOMETHING NEW EVERY DAY. The best way to do that? Become a certified INFOMANIAC* like me. I ♥ (that means L-O-V-E) information and I spend every spare minute finding out about all kinds of stuff.

What kinds of stuff? Stuff like...

1. The Cockroach Hall of Fame in Plano, Texas, features dead bugs dressed as celebrities and historical figures.

2. Candy makers manufacture 90 million chocolate Easter bunnies every year. And...

3. Ancient Romans used crushed mouse brains as toothpaste.

If you're still reading, you're probably an infomaniac, too, so you should know: Your brain is GROWING as you read. (Don't worry. It will still fit inside your skull.)

WARNING! Without a steady supply of information, infomaniacs may experience BRAIN SHRINKAGE. To guard fellow infomaniacs from this dire fate, I have developed a (not yet) patented TWO-STEP-BRAIN-EXPANDING-PROCESS.

STEP 1: Take my Infomaniac's Test (next page).
STEP 2: Read and complete this Infomaniac's Do-It-Yourself Diary.

INFOMANIAC'S TEST

For each question, circle "yes" or "no."

1. Do you want to know WHO invented marshmallow PEEPS? Yes / No

2. Do you want to know WHICH monkeys floss their teeth? Yes / No

3. Do you care WHY a woman with $100 million in the bank never washed her undies? Yes / No

4. Is your brain itching to start looking up answers instead of answering more questions? Yes / No

If you circled "yes" three or more times, you are definitely an infomaniac.

ONE MORE FACT: My best friend is a boy. (I know...embarrassing, but what can you do?) His name is John, and he's an infomaniac, too. In fact, he thinks he's the KING OF THE INFOMANIACS (questionable). He also thinks that, when he grows up, he will become the infomaniacal genius behind a best-selling trivia series called UNCLE JOHN'S BATHROOM READERS.

Why does he think that? A time-traveling lab rat named Dwayne told him. (I know...I know.) Anyway, John is looking for infomaniacs to join a trivia research team called The Bathroom Readers' Institute. I'm thinking about joining, but if YOU want to join, you'll need training. Here's how:

1) Complete the D-I-Y pages in this diary.

2) Fill out the Certificate of Completion at the back of this book.

3) Tear it out (or photocopy it) and mail it in!

4) Uncle John (my best friend after he loses all his hair and becomes an old bald guy) will send you an OFFICIAL BRI MEMBERSHIP CARD.

GO WITH THE FLOW!

This is me!

This is my pet chameleon, Iggie. She can look both ways at the same time and change color in 20 seconds flat!

This is my best friend, John, and his snoozy dog, Porter.

Stuff About Me

🐛 I live in New Jersey in a house so old George Washington once slept in it. (I am NOT kidding!)

🐛 I collect *Amazing Stories* magazine. My favorites were published in 1926. Back then they cost 25 cents. I found tales by Jules Verne, Edgar Allen Poe, and H.G. Wells all in a single issue. Now THAT'S amazing!

🐛 Mom says "You can never have too much of a good thing." Wrong! I once ate a whole pint of strawberries and broke out in HIVES. Mom made me soak in a baking-soda bath until my entire body looked like a big red prune. (Ugh!)

🐛 I am nearsighted (I see things up close really well but faraway things are fuzzy). Some of the less original boys at school call me "Four Eyes." NOTE TO THOSE BOYS: Given my superior intelligence, I may grow up to be your boss and I have a lo-o-ong memory.

Stuff About You

NiNCOMPOOP TEST

Why is it that some kids do smart things and other kids act like complete NINCOMPOOPS? I have devised this test to help you determine for yourself whether or not you're on the slippery slope to nincompoopage.

1. Have you ever stuck anything (besides toast) into a toaster to see what would happen? What? Why? And what happened?

2. If you could release any kind of insect or animal in your school, what would you release? Why?

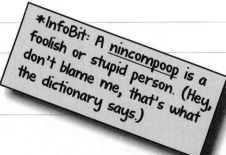

*InfoBit: A nincompoop is a foolish or stupid person. (Hey, don't blame me, that's what the dictionary says.)

3. If you had to mix together two things that are in your refrigerator and eat them, what would you mix?

4. Would you rather wear a grass skirt and dance in front of your class or eat a live frog?

5. If you had an anti-matter motor, what would you do with it?

6. Have you ever been tricked into doing something stupid? What? And who tricked you?

7. Where do penguins live?

DON'T CROSS ME!

Q: What do you get when you cross a school of fish with a herd of elephants?

A: Swimming trunks!

Okay, okay...elephant-fish hybrids don't exist (yet), but a bunch of other animal crosses do. The most famous one I've discovered so far? The **LIGER**. That's what you get when you cross a lion dad with a tiger mom (If the dad is a tiger and the mom is a lion, it's a **TIGON**). Ligers can weigh up to 1,000 pounds, making them the biggest felines alive today.

Some animal hybrids, like mules (donkeys crossed with horses) and beefalos (cattle crossed with bison), were bred for specific purposes. Mules were bred for carrying heavy loads. Beefalos, I'm sorry to report, were bred for dinner. I'm also sorry to report that crossbreeds don't have predictable temperaments. Ever heard the phrase "stubborn as a mule"? Crossbred species may also threaten the existence of natural species. So when elephant-fish are the new kings of the ocean, remember, you heard it here first!

D-I-Y ANimals

Q: What would you get if you crossed a chicken with a Komodo dragon?

A: A _____ .

Draw your new animal here.

Q: What would you get if you crossed a sheep with an electric eel?

A: A _____ .

Draw your new animal here.

Q: What would you get if you crossed a butterfly with a hippopotamus?

A: A _____ .

Draw your new animal here.

LuNch Lady Gets the Sack

Dear Lunch Lady,

You are required to attend a disciplinary hearing on May 14 at 2:30 p.m. The main items to be discussed at the hearing are as follows:

1. Feeding Pork to Muslim Students.

You should be aware that the disciplinary action taken could include termination of employment.

Sincerely,
The Principal

WRite Back!

Can you believe it? That letter was sent to a REAL lunch lady in England. And she was REALLY fired. Here's what she said: "I respect all of the children's beliefs, religions, and meal choices. This was just one mistake. I think firing me was really harsh."

Of course, there are two sides to every story. If you were the girl who found pork on her plate, what would you say to the lunch lady?

Dear Lunch Lady,

Sincerely,

*InfoBit: In England, to get the sack means to be fired from your job.

Super-Dooper Plumbing Maze

My best friend, John, keeps asking dumb riddles like, "What happens to a lab rat when you flush it?" If you don't know the answer, it's at the end of this maze.

It goes down the Dwayne!
(Drain...get it? Yeah, I thought so.)

Your Plumbing Maze

Your turn! START your maze with a riddle and END it
with the riddle's answer.

That's Awesome!

Carly Schuna of Madison, Wisconsin, says she's not naturally athletic but she LOVES doing tricks on the German wheel. Imagine two really big steel rings joined together by a set of parallel steel bars. Now picture a person inside the wheel, using those parallel bars to do tricks. Carly says the German wheel has made her stronger than she ever thought she could become. "This crazy apparatus makes me happy every day of my life!" Carly says. Here is Carly's drawing of one of her favorite tricks, the dancing flamingo!

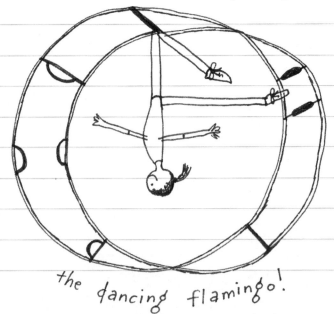

the dancing flamingo!

Be Awesome!

Your turn! Draw yourself doing something awesome.

Invent-o-Mat

My handy-dandy Invent-O-Mat (patent pending) is easy to use. Just choose items below. Stuff them into the top of the machine and turn the crank.

nuts & bolts	snake skin	lightbulb
rubber bands	world map	wire
bent fork	screws	Barbie doll head
rotten egg	gears	small motor
dirty sock	broken watch	empty soda can

Hey, Four Eyes!

D-I-Y Comic

It's your turn! Write and draw your own comic in the panels provided...with or without PI or PIE!

Ask an Expert

This morning, I had a question about a noise I'd been hearing. I tapped on the newspaper my mom hides behind at breakfast and asked her.

ME: Something is going "tap-tap-tap" inside my bedroom wall. What could it be?

MOM: "How should I know? Ask your father."

DAD: "I have no idea. Ask Grampie."

GRAMPIE: "What? Do I look like some kind of expert?"

To be honest, he didn't. So I asked Rita Rat-o-Rooter, the lady who gets rid of pests in our building.

RITA RAT-O-ROOTER:
Hmmm...could be red squirrels or gray squirrels or flying squirrels or mice or chipmunks. Could be rats, of course. Rats in the walls. Zoiks!

Anyways, kid, every one of those critters likes to store food and build nests in the walls.

Squirrel   Flying Squirrel   Mouse   Chipmunk

ME: So which one do you think it is?

RITA: Depends.

ME: On what?

RITA: On when you hear them. Mice, rats, and flying squirrels are nocturnal*. The rest are daytimers.

ME: I hear them at night.

RITA: So...most likely you have mice or rats or flying squirrels in your walls.

ME: Uhmm.... So which one?

RITA: What? Do I look like some kinda expert?

---

*InfoBit: <u>Nocturnal</u> means awake and active at night.

You Ask Experts

Your turn! Choose your five most pressing questions and find experts to answer them. (**WARNING**: Ask parents or grandparents at your own risk.)

YOU:

YOUR EXPERT:

YOU:

YOUR EXPERT:

YOU:

YOUR EXPERT:

YOU:

YOUR EXPERT:

YOU:

YOUR EXPERT:

Underwear Stuff

All of the boys in my class have *Fruitoftheloomophobia*. OK. I made up that term, but there's got to be a psychological reason for why boys always crack up if someone says "underwear." It's just stuff you wear under your other stuff, after all. This list includes REAL reasons to laugh at underwear.

🌀 During California's beach cleanup one year, crews found two phone booths, a plastic eyeball, half a bowling ball, a check written to Taco Bell for $8.78, Dracula teeth, and a pair of Scooby-Doo UNDERWEAR.

🌀 The astronauts aboard Gemini 7 flew home wearing only their long UNDERWEAR.

🌀 A multi-millionaire named Hetty Green NEVER washed her UNDERWEAR. Why not? She said it cost too much. (She had $100 million in the bank.)

YOUR UNdie stuff

List the weirdest stories you know about UNDERWEAR.

❤

❤

❤

❤

❤

❤

❤

Bug Body Parts

I've been thinking about becoming an entomologist. (That's a bug scientist.) Insects are super cool. They're kind of like aliens, with weird body parts that do unexpected things. A bug scientist named Roy Plotnick says insects have ears on every part of their bodies EXCEPT on their heads. Here's an **INFOMANIAC'S TEST:** Match each insect with its ear location.

INSECT	EAR LOCATION
Cricket	Knees
Tachinid fly	Thorax
Locust	Front legs
Katydid	Chin
Moth	Abdomen

MY FAVORITE BUG QUOTE: "We hope that, when the insects take over the world, they will remember with gratitude how we took them along on all our picnics."–Richard Vaughan

ANSWERS: Abdomen-Cricket, Chin-Tachinid fly, Front legs-Katydid, Thorax-Moth, Knees-Locust

More Body Parts

I like to think about why animals might need weird body parts. What do you think?

❦ **ONE REASON** an octopus might need eight legs is to divide a big cake into eight perfectly equal portions. What are some other reasons?

❦ **ONE REASON** a puffer fish might need spikes is to skewer some marshmallows for roasting. What are some other reasons?

❦ **ONE REASON** a lobster might need gigantic claws is to crush and eat a walnut. What are some other reasons?

 **YOUR FAVORITE BUG QUOTE:**

The Case of the Missing Chameleon

The First Nerd

Most etymologists* agree that the word "nerd" was invented by Dr. Seuss. Yep. The green eggs and ham guy. He used "nerd" in his 1950 book *If I Ran the Zoo* to describe a weird-looking imaginary zoo animal. Before long, people started using the word to mean "a smart but socially awkward person." Nerd has also come to mean "a single-minded expert in a particular field."

Chances are, I'll be a nerd when I grow up just like I am now. All I can say is, it's better than being a "geek." Why? Because the original geeks were carnival performers who bit off the heads of live chickens. Think I'm kidding? Look it up!

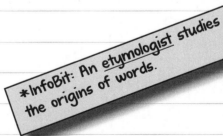

*InfoBit: An etymologist studies the origins of words.

Nerd Test

Can girls be nerds? There's only one way to find out!

COLOR IN ONE BUBBLE FOR EACH QUESTION.

1. Which is bigger?
- ⬤ your shoe size
- ⬤ your IQ
- ⬤ your comic book collection

2. Which do you know more about?
- ⬤ computers
- ⬤ hit TV shows
- ⬤ pop music stars

3. Which of these is NOT an element?
- ⬤ krypton
- ⬤ neon
- ⬤ snozzcomber

4. What's the grossest thing in your closet?
- ⬤ your dirty PJs
- ⬤ a Petri dish
- ⬤ a dissected frog

5. Which is your favorite game?
- ⬤ Mouse Trap
- ⬤ Chess
- ⬤ Twister

6. Which job would be more fun?
- ⬤ Paleontologist
- ⬤ BRI researcher
- ⬤ Rock Star

Are you a nerd? If you are, you can figure it out from your answers. If you can't...well, there's your answer!

Marti's Super-Colossal Fact Attack

The craziest facts I discovered this week:

🦃 A group of greyhounds is called a "leash" of greyhounds.

🦃 The world's heaviest turkey weighed 86 lbs. and was the size of a German shepherd.

🦃 Albert Einstein's eyes are being kept in a safe in New York City.

🦃 45% of Americans don't know that the Sun is a star (Did you?).

🦃 One plop of elephant poop can feed and house 7,000 beetles.

🐛 Raw termites taste like pineapple. (If you decide to taste-test this fact, please note the results below.)

🐛 In the Netherlands, peanut butter is called pindakaas ("peanut cheese").

🐛 Chewbacca's voice in Star Wars is a combination of sounds from a bear, a badger, a walrus, and a camel.

🐛 Some monkeys in Thailand teach their babies to floss their teeth.

🐛 Alaska has more outhouses than any other U.S. state.

RAW TERMITE TASTE TEST

Do raw termites taste like pineapple?

If you answered "no", please write what they taste like here:

YouR Facts

Create your own super-colossal fact list.

_____

_____

_____

_____

_____

_____

_____

_____

_____

_____

_____

_____

Dream On!

The other night, I had a horrible nightmare. I got a report card full of straight As...but they were all A minuses! (The horror...) I was so freaked out I couldn't go back to sleep. So I looked up dream facts:

- ❤ Everyone dreams.
- ❤ Most people over age 10 have four to six dreams every night.
- ❤ Parts of your brain shut down during dream sleep to rest and recharge. Other parts stay awake and cook up crazy situations that would never happen.
- ❤ Eighty percent of dreams are in color.
- ❤ Dreams are the brain's way of processing and understanding new information. So if you stop for a nap while studying, you'll learn more.
- ❤ Your muscles completely relax during dream sleep. It's called "sleep paralysis" and that's why you don't get up and act out your dreams.
- ❤ People around the world dream about school, falling, being attacked, and being frozen with fear.

Dream Generator

Pick a SETTING, a CHARACTER, and an ACTIVITY.
Make up a dream involving all three.

SETTING	CHARACTER	ACTIVITY
Farm	Dragon	Cooking
Lunchroom	Amoeba	Jogging
Zoo	Your crush	Brushing teeth
Science lab	Buffalo	Skydiving
Mall	Unicorn	Wrestling
Desert	Teddy bear	Dancing
School	Aliens	Camping

YOUR DREAM:

2dO b4 i'm 2Old

Yesterday, I asked my great-uncle Carmine why he has more hair growing out of his nose than on his head. "It's a sign of aging, young lady!" he said. "By the way, have you seen my teeth?" (I found them at the bottom of my cereal bowl...after I'd eaten my cereal.) That's when I decided to make a list of THINGS 2DO BEFORE I GET 2OLD to do them.

- Bungee jump off the Victoria Falls Bridge in Zambia.
- Run for President of the United States (and win).
- See a moonbow at Yosemite Falls.
- Build a house from old bottles.
- Help guard sea turtle eggs in Costa Rica.
- Visit all seven continents.
- Live in a treehouse for a year.
- Explore a shipwreck and look for treasure.
- Hunt for dinosaur bones in Mongolia's Gobi Desert.
- Invent false teeth that STAY IN YOUR MOUTH.

YOUR 2do List

Nona Josephina says getting old's not so bad. "The alternative is worse," she told me. "What do you mean?" I asked. "Croaking," she said. On that note, write your own 2DO BEFORE YOU CROAK list!

☞

☞

☞

☞

☞

☞

☞

DOWN the DWAYNe

STARRING...IGGIE THE KILLER CHAMELEON!

Sometimes I like to draw comics. But I don't always finish them. So feel free to add words and pictures.

infomania Central

My best friend, John, talks to a time-traveling lab rat named Dwayne. (I've never actually seen Dwayne, but time travel is theoretically possible, so who knows?) Dwayne says that one day John will head up the BATHROOM READERS' INSTITUTE. It's some kind of research institute for infomaniacs like me.

I live in New Jersey (so does John). But Dwayne says the BRI is in Oregon. John wants me to promise that, after I graduate from college, I will move to Oregon to become Head Infomaniac at the BRI. Sounds like fun, but right now my future goals include:

❦ Working in CALIFORNIA as a movie stunt woman.
❦ Becoming a spy. (My location will be so TOP SECRET that I might not even know where I am).
❦ Breeding chameleons in Madagascar.
❦ Digging up bones as a bioarcheologist. (Somewhere....)

> *InfoBit: A bioarcheologist studies skeletal remains at archaeological sites.

YOUR MOVE

It's your turn! Where will you live when you grow up?
Choose what you like best at each level and follow the
arrows to the next level. When you reach the bottom
of the page, turn the page to find your future home.

Welcome to...

Guess this explains how I ended up in Oregon!

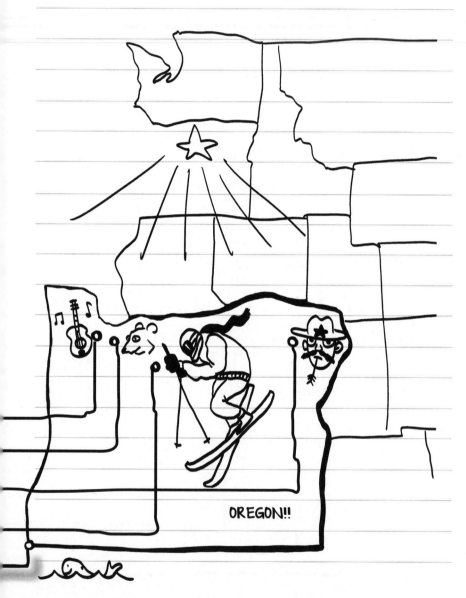

OREGON!!

Oregonia!

Don't like the results? Draw a line to where you'd
rather live as a grown-up. Draw pictures to
show why you'd rather live there.

Are You Kidding?

This is drool. Drool got on the page because my mouth is hanging open in disbelief. I just read a newspaper obituary (that's a fancy way to say "death announcement") about a famous Australian author named Colleen McCullough. She was Australia's best-selling author EVER. She wrote 25 books, including one that sold more than 30 MILLION copies. Her bestseller was made into a movie and a TV mini-series. She was also a neurophysiologist (an expert in the science of the electrical behavior of the nervous system). Oops! More drool...sorry.

Why is my mouth hanging open? Because the reporter wrote, "Plain of feature, and certainly overweight, she was, nevertheless, a woman of wit and warmth." Here's the thing: an obituary is supposed to be a mini-biography. Basically, the story of someone's life. So why is the reporter talking about her looks? That obituary reminds me of the nincompoopish boys at school who call me "four eyes."

I'm not the only one who thinks women deserve more respect. After that obituary was published, people posted ridiculous obits for themselves online. They wanted to show how ridiculous the Australian newspaper was to focus on McCullough's LOOKS, not her BOOKS.

One of my favorite authors—Neil Gaiman, who wrote the super-creepy *The Graveyard Book*—wrote this ridiculous obit for himself: "Although his beard looked like someone had glued it on and his hair would have been unconvincing as a wig, he married a rock star."

Here's my ridiculous obit: "Although she sprouted four eyes at age five, by age 16 Martina Fartiamo had changed diaries forever with her invention of the Instant Diary Drool Evaporator." ZAP!

YOUR TURN

Write your own ridiculous obituary here:

Although _____

[fill in the blanks]

_____

she _____

[fill in the blanks]

_____

_____ .

CRAZED COLLECTORS

You won't believe what I just found out! Russia's Peter the Great had a "kunstkammer." (That's a Chamber of Curiosities.) Guess what he kept inside? TEETH! How did he get the teeth? He pulled each one from the mouths of people he admired. (With admirers like that, who needs enemies?)

Peter the Great isn't the only odd collector in history. A Philadelphia doctor collected medical oddities. The weirdest? The thorax* of John Wilkes Booth, the guy who assassinated Abraham Lincoln. A man in California collects PEZ dispensers. The rarest? A "Make a Face" PEZ from the 1970s. You know, like Mr. Potato Head with attachable face parts? It was discontinued after kids kept eating the face parts along with the PEZ.

*InfoBit: Thorax is another word for chest. The lungs and heart are inside it.

What do I collect? *Amazing Stories* magazines (see page 10), harmonicas, and *Lost in Space* bubblegum card packs. My favorite is "The Awesome Menace" card.

You Collect!

If you had a Chamber of Curiosities, what would YOU collect? Draw your stuff here.

Catching Crooks

Statistically, women choose crime as a career far less often than men. (Whew!) But if you've even considered a life of crime, beware. Your own body parts leave behind evidence that can convict you in a court of law.

Personally, I have never considered a life of crime. Why not? First: I'm an INFOmaniac, not a KLEPTOmaniac. Second: fingerprints! Fingerprints are completely unique—even if you're an identical twin. So are toe prints, footprints, palm prints, and even...tongue prints.

Police don't sweep crime scenes for tongue prints (yet). And there's no International Tongue Print Database (yet). But a team of Chinese scientists has already created 3-D scans of more than 100 people's tongues. So it's just a matter of time until your tongue can turn you in!

Your Tongue Print

Iggie's tongue print looks like one of those paper party whistles that roll-out when you blow them. Mine looks like the heel print of a cowgirl boot. What about yours? Now's the time to find out!

1. Dry your tongue by blotting it with a paper towel.

2. Pour a small amount of food coloring into a very shallow dish.

3. Press your tongue onto the dish, moving it back and forth to get food coloring onto all sides.

4. Press your tongue here.

Teacher Sayings

My teacher has all these weird sayings like "Where there's smoke there's fire." Well, I'm here to tell you...that's not true. Every morning smoke comes out of our toaster. Why? Because Mom has burned the toast (again!). So far there hasn't been ANY fire. I've been logging in Miss Kawolski's sayings all year and feel confident that none of them can be proven scientifically.

- It's always darkest before the dawn.
- A watched pot never boils.
- Two heads are better than one.
- Every cloud has a silver lining.
- Two's company, three's a crowd.
- Better late than never.
- The early bird catches the worm.
- An apple a day keeps the doctor away.

Mixed-up Sayings

As far as I'm concerned, the sayings teachers say are fair game. Mix up the underlined endings from page 64 or make up your own!

It's always darkest _____

_____

A watched pot _____

_____

Two heads are _____

_____

Every cloud has _____

_____

Two's company, three's _____

_____

Better late than _____

_____

The early bird _____

_____

An apple a day _____

Over the Moon

Q: When does the moon need to take out a loan?

A: When it's down to its last quarter.

I decided to collect moon jokes. So far, I've only found two, so I filled the rest of the space with moon facts.

MOON FACT: The moon is freezing. And burning up. Temperatures on the moon's surface can span more than 500 degrees in a single day. In the middle of the day, it sometimes gets up to 250 degrees Fahrenheit. At night, it can drop down to -387 degrees.

MOON FACT: Mercury and Venus are the only "moonless" planets. Earth has just one moon, but both Saturn and Jupiter have more than 50. (Zoiks!)

MOON FACT: Not all moons are round. Earth's moon is kind of egg-shaped. Some scientists say Hyperion, one of Saturn's moons, is shaped like a hamburger patty.

MOON FACT: There's no sound, weather, wind, or clouds on the moon. (Which would make the moon very boring if not for the next fact.)

MOON FACT: A 3-foot jump on Earth would carry you 18 feet, 9 inches, on the moon.

MOON FACT: The moon is moving away from the Earth at the rate of about 1/8 inch a year.

MOON FACT: President John F. Kennedy pushed for NASA to put a man on the moon. That happened in 1969. But a man on the moon wasn't the president's first choice. He wanted NASA to send a man to MARS!

Q: What did the critic say about the restaurant on the moon?

A: The food's great but it has no atmosphere.

YOUR MOON FACT:

MOON
Observer's Log

An hour after sunset every night for a week, go outside and look up at the sky.

Night 1

DATE:

Draw the moon here. What else do you see?

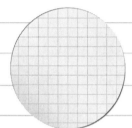

Night 2

DATE:

Draw the moon here. What else do you see?

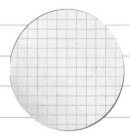

Night 3

DATE:

Draw the moon here.
What else do you see?

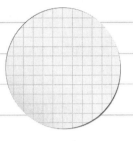

Night 4

DATE:

Draw the moon here.
What else do you see?

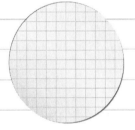

Night 5

DATE:

Draw the moon here.
What else do you see?

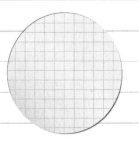

Night 6

DATE:

Draw the moon here.
What else do you see?

 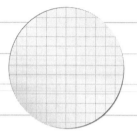

Night 7

DATE:

Draw the moon here.
What else do you see?

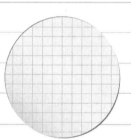

MARTI'S JOKE LOG

Q: Which is more useful, the sun or the moon?

A: The moon, because the sun only shines in the daytime when it's light anyway.

YOUR MOON JOKES

So far, I've found two moon jokes. Write your favorite moon jokes here. Maybe Dwayne the time-traveling lab rat can bring them to me in the past.

Q:

A:

Q:

A:

Q:

A:

Q:

A:

BaLANCiNg Act

My teacher Miss Kawolski just announced the date for this year's talent show. (Super. My biggest talent is matching my socks after doing laundry.) To get everyone excited about

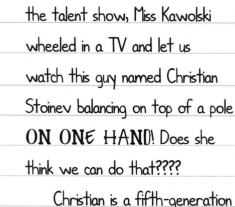

the talent show, Miss Kawolski wheeled in a TV and let us watch this guy named Christian Stoinev balancing on top of a pole **ON ONE HAND!** Does she think we can do that????

Christian is a fifth-generation acrobat. Acrobatics are in his DNA. To top it off, Christian has an adorable sidekick—a Chihuahua named Scooby who can walk on his front paws. (Hmmm...Maybe Iggie can perform in the talent show instead of me. He can change colors in two-minutes flat and hang from his tail.)

Christian says developing a skill or talent is all about not quitting. "Keep going until you get it," he says. "It's not going to come easy. If it did, everybody would do it!"

Practice Log

You probably don't have hand balancing skills like Christian Stoinev, but neither did he at age 10 when he first started. Choose a talent or skill to practice for a few minutes every day. Record your progress here.

Day 1:

Day 10:

Day 20:

Day 30:

Day 60:

Day 120:

Day 365:

Cryptid Guide

Last summer, I joined the Girl Guides. Why? Because I read a book called *Tales of the Cryptids*. Ever since, I've been taking the necessary steps to prepare for coming nose-to-nose with a CRYPTID*. In Girl Guides I learned to tie knots, make animal traps, and disguise my scent using Eau de Skunk. As part of my cryptid preparedness, I put together this descriptive guide.

CHUPACABRA: This cryptid's hard to pin down. It has been seen in South America. Some people say it has smooth skin. Others report reptilian skin or short, spiked, gray fur. It probably has fangs but might also have wings. Everyone agrees on one thing: the chupacabra sucks blood out of farm animals. I like chupacabra's nickname: "The Goat Sucker."

*InfoBit: A <u>cryptid</u> is a creature whose existence has not been proven (yet).

BIGFOOT: This big, hairy, bipedal (two-footed) ape-man has been spotted in the Pacific Northwest. He's about 8 or 9 feet tall, and leaves behind 15-inch footprints. Bigfoot's cold-weather cousin, the Yeti, hangs out in the snow-covered mountains of Tibet and Nepal.

THE WHIRLING WUMPUS:

The wumpus looks like Taz-the Tasmanian Devil from Looney Tunes cartoons-except, it's 7 feet tall! It hides in forests. When a logger comes along, it rears up on its powerful hind legs and spins so fast it becomes nearly invisible. The logger gets sucked into the whirling vortex, beaten to a pulp, and sprayed all over the surrounding vegetation.

NANDI BEAR: The forested mountains of eastern Africa are the supposed home of this supposed creature, whose name is taken from the Nandi people of Kenya. It's been described as about four feet tall at the shoulders, with reddish-brown fur. Its forelegs are longer than its hind legs, making it look more like a hyena than a bear. The Nandi Bear eats only one thing: the brains of its victims (Zoiks! It's Zombie Bear!). Sightings have been reported for hundreds of years. Some cryptozoologists say it may be a surviving *Pachycrocuta brevirostris,* or "giant hyena." Paleontologists say those went extinct 500,000 years ago.

MONGOLIAN DEATH WORM:

Never walk barefoot across the sands of Mongolia's Gobi Desert. Locals say a gigantic earthworm lives beneath the sand. This monster worm can projectile-spit venom. And if that's not scary enough, the death worm is covered in slime that can *KILL YOU* with a single touch.

THE **SNOW WASSET**: Like

an otter, but wa-a-a-ay bigger, this cryptid hibernates (snoozes) through the hot summer months. After the first snowfall, the snow wasset wakes up starving! For the rest of the winter it prowls beneath the snow. When it senses a meal (rabbits, squirrels, and even wolves are fair game) it pops up and gobbles its prey down. (Yum!)

Your Cryptids

It's your turn! Describe and draw pictures of unbelievable (but possibly real) creatures you've seen or heard about.

Draw your cryptid here.

CREATURE:
DESCRIPTION:

Draw your cryptid here.

CREATURE:
DESCRIPTION:

Draw your cryptid here.

CREATURE:
DESCRIPTION:

CREATURE:
DESCRIPTION:

Draw your cryptid here.

CREATURE:
DESCRIPTION:

Draw your cryptid here.

CREATURE:
DESCRIPTION:

Draw your cryptid here.

CREATURE:
DESCRIPTION:

Draw your cryptid here.

magic or MURDER?

Last week, I went with my friend John to a magic show. The best part? The magician sawed his assistant in half. Or at least, that's what it looked like. John's mother said it was just an optical illusion.

WHAT I SAW:

1. The assistant stretched out in a box and the magician shackled her down.

2. He closed the box and sawed it in half.

3. She screamed. (I screamed, too!)

4. Then the magician pulled the box apart to show he'd really sawed her in half. (I screamed again.)

5. Then he pushed the box back together, took the blade out, and opened the box to reveal the assistant all in one piece without a drop of blood on her.

What the heck? I had to find out what was going on, so I did a bit of sleuthing. Turns out, as soon as the magician closes the box, the assistant wiggles out of the shackles and tucks her knees up to her chest. She stays that way while the magician saws the box in half and separates the halves. (Since her crouch takes up only half the box, she never gets sawed.) After the magician puts the box back together, she extends her legs again and gets back into the shackles for the big reveal. **TA-DA!**

HARRY HOUDINI'S ESCAPE TRICK

Wondering how that magician's assistant got out of her bonds? Here's how legendary escape artist Houdini got loose:

1. While being tied up, make yourself as big as possible by inhaling and pushing your chest out.

2. Flex any muscles that are being tied up (Do it as sneakily as possible so as not to raise suspicion).

3. Now relax. You'll get at least a half an inch of slack in the ropes, which may be enough to wiggle yourself loose.

Go ahead! Give it a try. (But don't blame me if you have to yell for your mom, dad, or annoying sibling to untie you.)

How to Palm a Coin

My research into magic revealed one more magical secret: Here's how to palm a coin!

1. Open your hand and look at the coin. Touch your thumb to your pinkie finger. See the big fold in the middle of your hand? That's where you're going to store the coin.

2. Open your hand again and put the coin right in the middle of it.

3. Now flex the muscles in your palm, trying to grip the coin without making the rest of your hand look too weird. Can you keep the coin there and turn your hand over? Practice until you can!

magic & Movies!

My best friend, John, showed me the palmed coin trick. He
was a bit peeved when I figured it out right away. (Ha!)

What can you palm with no one noticing?
Make a list here:

❤
❤
❤
❤
❤

My favorite movie is *The Mad Magician*. It's a horror film
from 1954. List your favorite movies here:

❤
❤
❤
❤
❤

My Future Empire

As you know, my best friend, John, believes he will grow up to become the leader of a vast and tentacled trivia empire. I'm beginning to think anyone who listens to a time-traveling lab rat has to be nuts. In fact, I'm pretty sure I'm the one who will someday found an empire. Instead of a time-traveling rat, my closest advisers will be a sentient lion and a super-smart rhino.

My empire will probably be funded by the invention of the floating bubble car. I'll have to be very careful to keep my rhino adviser from bursting my bubble. (Ha!)

YOUR FUTURE EMPIRE

You have (at least) two possible futures:

1. You will join my team of super-sentient beings and help me to expand (Ha!) my bubble car empire, or...

2. You will create your own vast and tentacled empire.

DRAW YOUR FUTURE HERE.

What Do i See?

FUN FACT: I am a little colorblind. Well, to be more precise, I am "color vision deficient." That's a fancy way of saying that I can't always tell green from red. It makes the holiday season kind of confusing. (I can't tell Santa apart from the elves.)

To be truly colorblind, you have to be unable to see any colors at all outside of black and gray. (The technical name is *achromatopsia*.) Thankfully, that's not me! Here's what else I have found out:

❧ Color blindness is a lot more common in boys. Almost 10 percent of guys have it to some degree, but only 0.5 percent of girls do. (Lucky me!)

❧ Color blindness can lead to food poisoning. (Huh?) When you're colorblind, raw meat can look just about the same as cooked meat. (Ugh!)

❧ "Rods" and "cones" are the cells in your eyes that let you see. Rods detect light and cones detect color. To get a taste of colorblindness, go into a dark closet. The rods in your eyes will be working but the cones won't.

You See What?

Optometrists (otherwise known as eye doctors) have fancy tests to tell if you're colorblind or not. But even without those, you can get an idea of how good your color detection is. For each sentence, circle "yes" or "no."

- ❤ People are always telling me that my outfits clash or that my clothes don't match. (yes/no)
- ❤ Most pale colors just look like shades of white or gray. (yes/no)
- ❤ I can't always tell teams apart in a game of basketball or baseball because their jerseys all look the same to me. (yes/no)
- ❤ When someone asks me to draw or paint with a certain color, I have no idea which one to pick because a lot of them look alike to me. (yes/no)

Take your eye doctor's test to be sure, but three or more "yes" answers might mean you're a little colorblind like me!

Goofy GrownUps

Apparently, growing up doesn't necessarily make you smarter. My evidence?

❧ A man in India made it into the Guinness book of world records by letting his ear hair grow to 5.25 inches.

❧ A Florida woman covered her yard in mothballs, which—by the way—are toxic to plants and wildlife. Why'd she do it? To keep neighbors' dogs from pooing on her lawn.

❧ A man in London bought his girlfriend a $12,000 diamond engagement ring. He took it to a florist and had it placed inside a helium balloon. The balloon was attached by a string to a bouquet of flowers. As he left the shop, the string slipped out of his hand and the balloon (with the ring inside) floated away.

YOUR Goofy GROWNups

Log in the goofiest things your parents—or
other grownups in your life—have done.
(Is this fun, or what?)

❤

❤

❤

❤

❤

DiNo-scARiuM!

Some people think dino-mania is a boy thing. I disagree. Why? Because of Sue Hendrickson. Ms. Hendrickson is the paleontologist* who dug up the remains of the BIGGEST T. REX EVER FOUND! The dinosaur she discovered is called SUE (named after her, of course). If you're ever in Chicago, you can see Sue (the dino, not the paleontologist) at The Field Museum.

Here's my list of scary dinosaurs I would NOT want to meet on the street:

PLIOSAUR.

Pliosaur was a water creature with a skull as long as a human man is tall. It had a total body length of more than 40 feet. Pliosaurs mostly ate fish, but some pliosaur skeletons have been discovered with dinosaur remains in their stomachs. Paleontologist Richard Forrest says pliosaur was "probably the most fearsome predator that ever lived." WHY? Because they ripped apart dinos that got close to the shoreline and ATE THEM.

ANKYLOSAUR. Ankylosaur lived during the same time as T. rex, and whenever it was attacked, it made the predator's life as miserable as possible. In addition to being covered from head to toe in nature's toughest spikes and armor plates, the dino had a club as a tail. When whipped with enough force, the tail could gouge the skin of attackers and even crush their bones.

UTAHRAPTOR. According to the Dinosaur Museum in Dorchester, England, Utahraptor wins the title of all-time "fiercest dinosaur." It may not have been as big or as strong as predators like T. rex, but it had smarts on its side. (Speaking from experience, it can't hurt to have smarts on your side.) Utahraptor also had fingers and toes with foot-long claws. (Those can't hurt either...unless you're the prey.)

*InfoBit: A paleontologist is someone who studies animal and plant fossils.

Design-a-Raptor

In 2014, paleontologists digging in Venezuela discovered bones from a brand-new dinosaur, *Tachiraptor admirabilis*. Scientists think this raptor was about five feet long from nose to tail, that it had sharp teeth, and that it walked on two legs. It lived about 200 million years ago in a volcanically active region surrounded by valleys.

Based on that information, what do you think *Tachiraptor admirabilis* looked like? (Scales? Spikes? Feathers? A feather boa?)

What do you think it ate? (Hint: Probably not doughnuts.)

Where might it have slept at night?

How do you think it hunted and
defended itself from attacks?

DRAW YOUR RAPTOR IN THE SPACE BELOW.

Get Greek'd

Socrates was a really smart guy who lived in ancient Greece between 469 and 399 B.C. (Isn't it weird how dates went backward before the year A.D. 1?) Anyway, Socrates taught his students by asking lots and lots of questions. They probably thought he was just being obnoxious, but actually probing questions help you learn to think more clearly and deeply about things. Here are a few probing questions for all you budding infomaniacs!

What do you think is the most important thing you have done so far in life?

What makes you think that is true?

Sorry, I don't understand. Can
you give me a few examples?

Is that all? What haven't you told me yet?

Spaced Out Twins

I used to think time was pretty straightforward. When I looked at a clock, the seconds ticked forward one after another. If I said, "One Mississippi, two Mississippi" and so on, I could count the seconds pretty accurately.

That was before I heard Albert Einstein's ideas about "time dilation." Einstein thought time sped up or slowed down depending on how fast one thing was going in relation to another thing. Right now, you're probably thinking, "HUH?"

Here's an example: Let's say you have a set of identical twins. One of them grows up to be an astronaut and rockets into space. The other stays home on Earth. Time dilation means that time passes MORE SLOWLY for someone rocketing through space than for someone back home on Earth. While traveling the astronaut twin would age more slowly than the Earth-bound twin. When the astronaut twin returned to Earth, she'd be younger than her sister. How much younger? It depends. The faster and farther the astronaut few, the older her twin would be when she got home.

Which twin would you rather be, the one that ends up younger or the one that ends up older?

Why?

In theory, if you could travel faster than the speed of light (186,000 miles in a second), you could go backward in time. "When" would you go and what would you do?

Your Time Travels

Just because scientists haven't figured out how to time travel yet doesn't mean you can't make plans. Fill in the blanks with your own time-travel plans:

If I could speed to any time in the past, I would visit the year _____ so that I could

_____

_____

with _____ .

To change _____ ,
I would travel to the year_____ . When I got there, I would _____

_____

_____

_____

_____ .

The thing I regret most from my past is

_____

_____

_____ .

If I could travel back to that moment, I would

_____

instead of _____

_____ .

If I could speed 25 years into the future, I
would go to _____ ,
so that I could _____

_____ .

If I could speed 100 years into the future, I
would go to _____ ,
so that I could _____

_____

_____

_____ .

Shortz Tips!

I read somewhere that brains need exercise just like other parts of the body. One of my favorite ways to brain-train is to do crossword puzzles. Despite daily training, *The New York Times* puzzles still baffle me sometimes. I decided to ask crossword editor Will Shortz for some tips.

TIP 1 – Don't be afraid to guess.

TIP 2 – If you run into problems, erase and start over.

TIP 3 – If you're completely stuck, put the puzzle aside and come back later.

TIP 4 – Start with a Monday *NYTimes* puzzle (Mondays are the easiest).

TIP 5 – Always fill in an answer you are sure of first.

Once you get the hang of solving puzzles, try writing them. That can be a lot trickier (I'm still practicing).

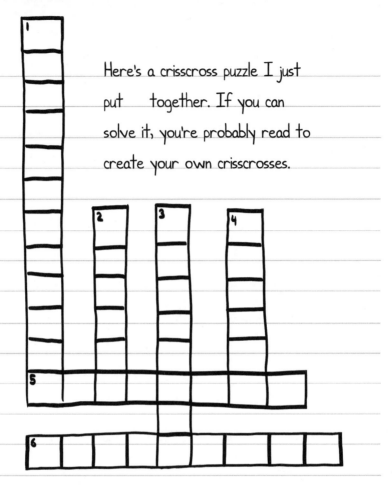

Here's a crisscross puzzle I just put   together. If you can solve it, you're probably read to create your own crisscrosses.

ACROSS
2.   An unusual Japanese monster.
6.   A witch's best subject in school.

DOWN
1.   Which goblin ate the Three Bears' porridge?
3.   What is a vampire's favorite fruit?
4.   The undead.
5.   After running a marathon, your feet are...

Answers: 1. Ghouldilocks, 2. Oddzilla, 3. Nectarine, 4. Zombie, 5. Dragon, 6. Spelling.

Be a Puzzler

Train for puzzle construction. Build your first crossword puzzle here!

1. Fill in the answers. Make sure that all the letters you use make words while reading both across and down. Black out any squares that you haven't filled with letters.

2. Number your answers, making separate lists for Across and Down. The first Across answer is 1, and so is the first Down answer. Write each number in the square for the first letter of that answer.

3. Write clues for your answers. Give the clues (and another grid, with the numbers and black squares in it but no answers) to your mom and see if she can solve it.

[Write your puzzle title on the line.]

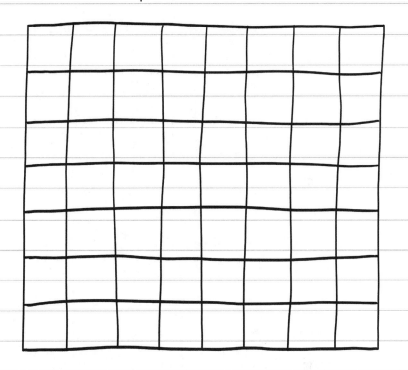

YOUR CLUES:

CRISSCROSS This

Want to try a few crisscross puzzles? All you need are words and clues. I've found puzzle-making to be easier if I choose a theme and come up with words to fit the theme. Use this theme list to get started.

PUZZLE THEMES

SCARY THINGS	GEMS AND ROCKS
BOOK CHARACTERS	SPORTS TEAMS
ANIMALS	REPTILES
SCHOOL STUFF	MYTHICAL CREATURES
THINGS IN MY BACKPACK	SPACE STUFF
FOREST THINGS	FAVORITE AUTHORS
MOVIE MONSTERS	COMIC BOOK HEROINES
FAIRYTALE STUFF	WACKY TOWN NAMES
GAME CHARACTERS	BUGS
TV VILLAINS	GIRL GENIUSES

YOur CrisscroSs

OK. Here's some space. Choose a theme (or two) and create your own crisscross(es).

Auto-robotics

This week, I'm reading about some of the world's first robots. They were called *automatons*. What's an automaton? It's a mechanical device made to look like a person. A set of coded instructions allows the machine to do whatever it is programmed to do.

Maybe you've heard of Maillardet's automaton. It was invented around 1810 by a Swiss watchmaker named Henri Maillardet. The watchmaker's automaton looked like the top half of a boy sitting behind a writing desk. The boy's body was welded into a machine filled with rotating disks that let it write (I am not kidding!) in two languages: French and English.

How? Those rotating disks worked sort of like a computer's read-only memory. They stored all the data needed for the robot to write—and even draw— in a creepily lifelike way. At the time Maillardet built his automaton, it had the largest memory of any mechanical device. Here's a question: If it had such a big memory, why wasn't it a GIRL automaton??? GEEZ!

Here's my version of one of the machine's drawings:

Wondering about that pudgy baby with the arrow? That's Cupid, the ancient Roman god of love. Cupid shoots arrows at people to make them fall in love. Roman myths are TWFW (Two Weird for Words).

i ♥ Robots

Maillardet's humanoid automaton inspired a book titled
The Invention of Hugo Cabret by Brian Selznick.
The book was made into a movie. If you haven't
read the book or watched the movie, what are you
waiting for?

    Now that you're back, draw your ideal robot here:

Now make a list of things your robot would do for you (make your bed, clean your chameleon's box, etc.):

1.

2.

3.

4.

5.

6.

7.

8.

9.

All's Fair in Science

D-i-y Mystery

Write and draw your own comic mystery.

Ladies First!

A lot of the history books I read seem to be just that: HIS-story. Sure, I'm interested in stuff guys have done, but I'm also interested in what GIRLS have done. Today, I'm into HERstory. Check it out!

❤ In 1770, Frenchwoman Isabel Godin des Odonais sailed 3,000 miles down the Amazon River from Peru to Brazil. That made her the first woman to cross South America from the Pacific to the Atlantic. She was the only member of her 42-person party to survive the fevers, accidents, and tribal attacks that plagued them the entire way.

❤ In 1871, Lucy Walker became the first woman to scale the legendary Matterhorn mountain in the Swiss Alps—and she did it wearing only a simple white cotton dress beneath her climbing harness.

❤ In 1936, a New York socialite named Ruth Harkness emerged from the remote highlands of Tibet with the first giant panda ever captured alive.

Your Firsts

The first time you do something adventurous is always amazing. Log in your AMAZING firsts here:

MY #1 FIRST

MY #2 FIRST:

MY #3 FIRST:

MY #4 FIRST:

MY #5 FIRST:

Stomach This!

Have you ever been forced to eat something TGFW (Too Gross for Words)? Once a week the lunch ladies at B.A. Bighead Elementary dish up Mystery Meat. What is it? It's a mystery. (Ha!)

Yesterday, I discovered that even professional chefs scarf down TGFW meals every once in a while. I asked a chef I know what the most disgusting thing he had ever eaten was.

"My mom used to make this soup with tripe in it when I was a kid," he said. "She tried to tell me tripe was a FISH. I looked it up in the dictionary and found out it was COW STOMACH. The pieces of stomach were wiggly and jiggly. It was like biting into gummy worms that tasted like rubber bands."

Um, eew...I may be an infomaniac, but I wish he'd kept that bit of information to himself!

What CaN U Stomach?

Write a detailed description of the most disgusting things you have ever eaten. For each one, include taste, smell, and how it felt in your mouth.

Cars of the Future

I like to imagine what cars will look like when I'm old enough to drive.

I'm counting on a bubble car. . .one that bobs along in the air. If someone runs into me, my bubble car will just bounce a bit and float away.

What would your dream car of the future look like? Draw it here:

Check what you'd like to have inside your car:

- ☐ hot chocolate machine
- ☐ video gaming device
- ☐ deflector shield
- ☐ ejector seats (for irritating riders)
- ☐ voice-activated phone
- ☐ nail polish applicator
- ☐ an endless supply of stickers

other _____

Draw the car you think your favorite superhero should be driving here:

Check the things your superhero's car should have:

- [ ] x-ray vision windshield
- [ ] non-skid monster truck tires
- [ ] instant hair dryer
- [ ] ejector seats (for bad guys)
- [ ] voice-activated phone
- [ ] seat for sidekick
- [ ] tire-grabbing glop sprayer

other _____

Oops!

I don't know about you, but I love spotting goofs, blunders, and bloopers like the ones below in news stories. They prove that adults make as many mistakes as kids do.

GOOF: The *Oprington News Shopper* gave the names of three children as "Gavin, 3, and 11-year-old twins Helen and ugh." (Poor ugh! And, yes, the twin's name was Hugh.)

HEADLINE BLOOPER:

VOLUNTEERS SEARCH FOR
OLD CIVIL WAR PLANES

PROBLEM: The world's first military plane was the 1909 Wright Military Flyer. The Civil War ended in 1865. (Guess no one told the news writer!)

BLUNDER: After an earthquake struck Alaska's Aleutian Islands, a TV news anchor said it was "a 7.2 magniturd earthquake."

Oops Collection

It's your turn to collect oops, goofs, blunders, and bloopers. You'll find lots of them on the Internet, but magazines, newspapers, and even books can be great sources for proof that grown-ups goof, too!

GOOFS:

BLUNDERS:

BLOOPERS:

My best friend, John, drew
this disgusting superhero.
I tried to stop him.

MAGNITURD

PONDER this!

Sometimes, instead of getting on the Internet to find answers to questions, I like to mull them over myself. It's your turn! What do you think?

 How can you tell a girl earthworm from a boy earthworm?

Will I really get zits if I eat chocolate or fried foods?

 What's really in a hot dog? (And does anyone really want to know?)

Why do some people stick out their tongues when they're concentrating on something?

Why do most kids hate liver and Brussels sprouts?

Why do cats' eyes shine in the dark?

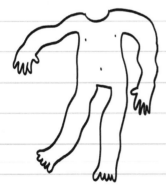

Why isn't our skin green or blue?

What might be living on your toothbrush?

Worst Advice Ever!

Lately, everyone wants to give me advice: my parents, my teacher, Nona Josephina—who calls me "Patatina" ("little potato") because she can't remember my name. Take a look at the stinkiest advice I've gotten so far.

ADVICE: "Stay the course."

THE STINK: Whenever Great Uncle Carmine sees someone about to give up he yells, "Stay the course!" I think staying the course only makes sense if you're headed in a sensible direction. If you're long boarding down a hill and you haven't learned to slide yet and the hill you're bombing is really steep and there's a crossroad filled with cars at the bottom—DO NOT STAY THE COURSE!

ADVICE: "If you keep raising your hand in class, everyone will think you're a know-it-all."

THE STINK: The substitute teacher told our class there were no numbers lower than zero. Guess he didn't like it when I told him about those pesky negative numbers.

ADVICE: "High school will be the best four years of your life, so enjoy it!"

THE STINK: It all goes downhill after age 18? That CAN'T be right!

ADVICE: "Respect your elders."

THE STINK: I get this one a lot. Nona Josephina uses it as an excuse for everything.

ADVICE: "Sticks and stones may break your bones but words will never harm you."

THE STINK: Obviously, the person who came up with this pearl had 1) not been called Four Eyes, Stupid, or Wimpy, etc..; and 2) never been hit over the head with a dictionary.

This Advice Stinks!

The smell scale rates stinky advice from garbage (stinky) to dirty diaper (stinkiest). ❤ List the advice people gave you below and check where it ranks on the smell scale.

ADVICE:

ADVICE:

ADVICE:

ADVICE:

ADVICE:

Fear Facts

Ever heard of Alexander the Great? Born in 356 B.C., he conquered most of the known world before his death at age 33. But that didn't stop him from being a scaredy-cat. That's right. Alexander suffered from AILUROPHOBIA: the fear of cats. One report says he actually FAINTED at the sight of a cat.

Whenever I get freaked out by my biggest fears, I remind myself that if Alexander didn't let being a scaredy-cat stop him, why should I?

MY #1 FEAR? ARACHNOPHOBIA (fear of spiders) J.K. Rowling, author of the Harry Potter books, is scared of spiders, too. She gave the same fear to the character Ron Weasley. When she discovered that Rupert Grint—the actor who plays Ron in the films—is afraid of spiders in real life, she felt bad for him. In the movies, Ron is in LOTS of scenes with spiders. (Shudder!)

MY #2 FEAR? COULROPHOBIA (fear of clowns)

Don't laugh. Painted white faces, grinning red lips, wild hair sprouting from balding heads...and those bulbous red noses! Talk about scary. And it's not just me. Dr. Brenda Wiederhold, a psychologist, says fear of clowns starts around age two, when kids start to get anxious about being around strangers. "At that age, children's minds are still developing and they're not always able to separate fantasy from reality." Think about that for a minute: if you didn't know that clowns are just people dressed up in silly suits, wouldn't YOU be scared?

MY #3 FEAR? LYGOPHOBIA (fear of the dark)

There are plenty of good reasons for being afraid of the dark. There could be gremlins in the closet or ghosts hovering beneath the ceiling or monsters under the bed. My teacher Ms. Kawolski says people who are afraid of the dark have over-active imaginations. That's me... over-active imagination girl! Last night I imagined that a gigantic spider with a big red clown nose was spinning a thread from the ceiling down to my head. (The horror!)

Fear Face-offs

When I start to feel scared, I imagine face-offs between things that scare me. For example, what would happen if a clown went up against a giant spider? How about a monster-size bee against the ghoul that lives in my closet? Here's what I think that would look like. (I think Buzzilla is going to win this sting-off.)

BUZZILLA VS. GHOULASH

Battle it Out!

Nothing could be safer than letting your fears do battle on paper. Name them, then draw them.

VS. _____

VS. _____

Animalia

This list contains three things I love: animals, numbers, and weirdness.

- The world's longest earthworms (found only in a small corner of Australia) can grow to as long as **12 FEET** and as thick as a soda can.
- Squids have the largest eyes in nature: up to **10 INCHES** across.
- The longest flying-squirrel flight on record is **300 FEET** (actually, they glide).
- By **AGE 15**, most tuna have swum more than a million miles.
- As a species, the platypus is **150 MILLION** years old.
- A woodpecker's beak moves at a speed of **14-16 MPH**.
- Alpaca wool comes in **22 NATURAL COLORS**. (I wish my hair had 22 colors in it!)

*InfoBit: <u>Animalia</u> is the group of living things that includes ALL ANIMALS.

YOUR ANIMALIA

Thud-ump...Thud-ump

Guess what? I like gym class. Why? Because I get
to do things that are considered "inappropriate" for
girls. My favorites: Throwing things, climbing on things,
competing against boys (and winning), and using my
"outdoor voice." I also learned from one of Mom's
magazines that exercise can even make you smarter.

HEART-PUMPING EXERCISE HELPS YOU:

- Think faster and more clearly.
- Do better on tests that require memorization.
- Increase problem-solving ability for math class.
- Learn vocabulary words up to 20 times faster.
- Be in a better mood all day long.

Sound good? To get these BRAIN benefits, work your
BODY for at least 30 minutes at least 3 times a week.

Get a Pulse!

FIND YOUR RESTING HEART RATE: Trace a path down your thumb to where your palm meets your wrist. Place two fingers there. When you feel your heartbeat, count the number of beats for 15 seconds and multiply by 4.

My resting heart rate is: _____

My heart rate after...

...jogging in place for 30 seconds? _____

...doing 20 jumping jacks? _____

...dancing for 1 full song? _____

...walking around the block? _____

...standing on one leg for 1 minute? _____

What's next? You're an infomaniac! Do some research to find your ideal exercise heart rate and try to hit it.

RESTING HEART RATES

Canary – 1,000 bpm (beats per minute)

Elephant – 30 bpm

Rat – 325 bpm

Whale – 20 bpm

Human kid – 90 bpm

Scrabble Challenge

It doesn't take a genius to guess that I am a Scrabble pro. In fact, I, Martina Fartiamo, am the reigning Scrabble Champion of B.A. Bighead Elementary. How'd I win the title? In a word: SYZYGY*. Think you know as much about the world's favorite word game as I do? Take my Scrabble Trivia Challenge.

1. Scrabble's original name was:
   A. Lexico
   B. Lotsa Letters
   C. Wordgrams

2. The inventor of Scrabble was named:
   A. Christopher Holmes
   B. Alfred Butts
   C. Tammy Nomenclature

*InfoBit: <u>Syzygy</u> [SIZ-i-jee] is an alignment of three celestial bodies.

3. There are _____ tiles in a Scrabble game. (As long as you haven't lost any.)

   A. 125

   B. 100

   C. 75

4. Scrabble is produced and sold in _____ different languages.

   A. 29

   B. 46

   C. 12

5. At Scrabble tournaments, _____ is banned.

   A. Talking

   B. Loud sighing

   C. Suspicious behavior

Big Word Collection

Want to be a Scrabble champ? Better come prepared. Start your word collection here. Collect words on the next page and use the point key below to tally up their point values. Then get ready to crush your opponents!

Example: BRAINIAC = 11 points

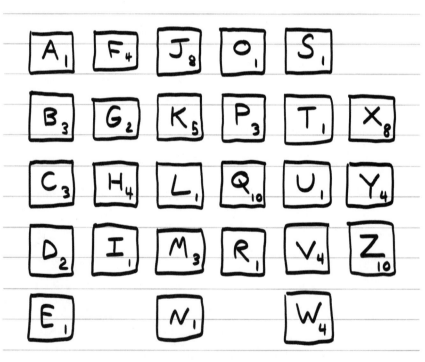

Word: _____ Points: _____

Word: _____ Points: _____

Word: _____ Points: _____

Word: _____ Points: _____

Word: _____ Points: _____

Word: _____ Points: _____

Word: _____ Points: _____

Word: _____ Points: _____

Word: _____ Points: _____

Word: _____ Points: _____

Word: _____ Points: _____

Word: _____ Points: _____

Word: _____ Points: _____

Word: _____ Points: _____

Word: _____ Points: _____

Word: _____ Points: _____

Word: _____ Points: _____

Word: _____ Points: _____

Word: _____ Points: _____

Word: _____ Points: _____

Word: _____ Points: _____

Tiger Trouble!

More Tiger Trouble

What happens after the B.A. Bighead team mascot shows up? Draw it here.

WUTs Out There?

My best friend, John, invited me to his house for movie night. We watched *War of the Worlds*. Ever since, he's been wondering if aliens are out there waiting to invade Earth. What do I think? WUTs (Weird Unexplained Things) happen! Take Roswell, for example. Haven't heard about Roswell? Read and learn.

WEATHER OR NOT: On July 4, 1947, a bright light shot across the sky over Roswell, New Mexico. It exploded and fell to earth on a ranch outside of town. Several people rushed to see what it was. What did they see? "An airplane without wings." They also saw three alien-looking bodies. Two were on the ground and one was visible through a hole in the side of the craft. Air Force officials issued a press release stating that a "flying disk" had crashed. But the next day...they asked for a "take back." It wasn't an alien ship after all, they said. It was...a weather balloon.

ALIEN TECH: In 1961, Colonel Philip Corso, of the U.S. Army Research and Development Department said, "Alien technology harvested from the infamous saucer crash in Roswell, New Mexico, led directly to the development of the integrated circuit chip, laser and fiber optic technologies, particle beams, electromagnetic propulsion systems, depleted uranium projectiles, stealth capabilities, and many others. How do I know? I was in charge!"

WUTS ON YOUR LIST?

We all see weird stuff. I'll share mine. You share yours!

💙 I saw a HUGE disk-shaped cloud hovering above Mt. Shasta, California.

💙 Walking to school one day, I saw a glowing red ball floating down my street.

💙 I was flying from New Jersey to Florida and saw a metallic object out the airplane window.

💙 _____

_____

_____

💙 _____

_____

_____

💙 _____

_____

_____

Draw an alien

After decades of investigation, scientists still have no idea what aliens might look like. If aliens are out there, what do you think they look like? **DRAW THEM BELOW.** Add something ordinary (like a chameleon or an giraffe) to your drawing for scale.

UFOs Unscrambled

Before you tell your friends about that UFO you saw make sure it's not—

_ _ _ _ _ (N V U S E)

or a _ _ _ _ _ _ (T E M R O E)

or _ _ _ _ _ _ _ _ _ (P E C A S) (K J N U)

or a _ _ _ _ _ (D O L U C)

or a _ _ _ _ _ _ _ _ _ _ _ _ (T R A E H W E) (O N L A B O L)

or you'll end up feeling really _ _ _ _ (M U B D).

ANSWERS: You're kidding, right? If you can't unscramble these how will you ever hope to outsmart the aliens when they land?

149

Origami Heroes

Last summer at Camp Wannafolda, I learned to make origami puppets. The arts and crafts counselor was an exchange student from Japan. She handed out beautiful patterned paper and showed us how to make puppets that looked like girls wearing pretty kimonos. Kimonos are cool, but if you start with plain white paper, you can decorate your puppets to look like superheroes! Just follow the steps below.

STEP 1: Take a sheet of paper and lay it longwise or shortwise on a table or desk.

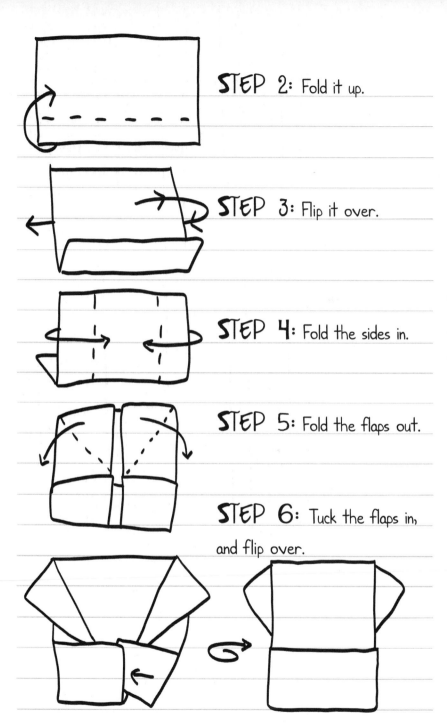

STEP 2: Fold it up.

STEP 3: Flip it over.

STEP 4: Fold the sides in.

STEP 5: Fold the flaps out.

STEP 6: Tuck the flaps in, and flip over.

NOTE: Before drawing on your puppet, turn the page!

Hero Faces

At Camp Wannafolda, I messed up a bunch of origami puppets trying to turn them into superheroes. Take my advice: Practice drawing costumes and faces here.

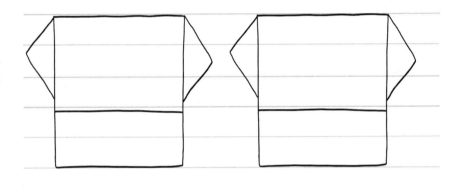

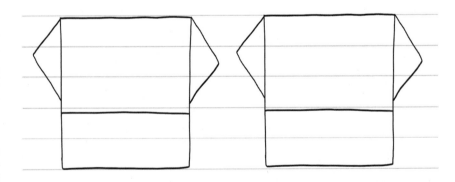

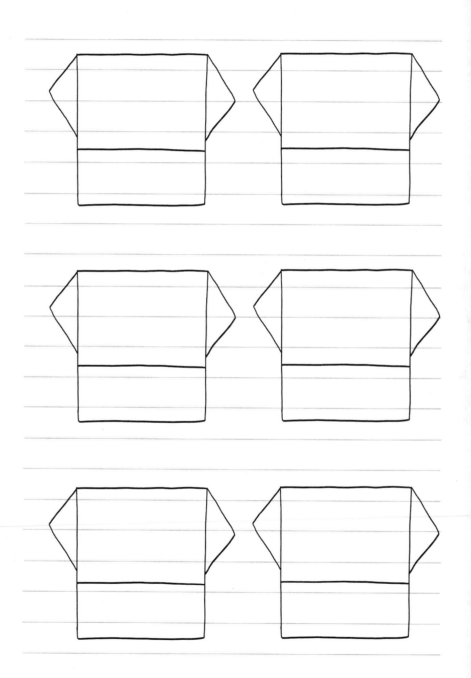

Useful Disguises

I've been doing research on disguises hoping to come up with a way to skulk around B.A. Bighead Elementary without being noticed. Why? I'm on the lookout for news to put into the *Bighead Digest*, a 'zine I plan to write, illustrate, print, and sell. Here are three disguises from history that worked (at least...at first).

❤ **DISGUISE** #1: Native Americans

❤ **THE STORY:** Ever heard of the Boston Tea Party? It wasn't really a tea party. It was a protest against a tax placed on tea by the British government. In 1773, a group of Massachusetts colonists disguised themselves as Mohawk Indians. They crept aboard British tea ships docked in Boston Harbor and dumped 342 chests of tea overboard. The chests held about 45 tons of tea, so it took them three hours to dump it all. In today's money, the tea was worth $1,000,000.

♥ DISGUISE #2: Trees

♥ THE STORY: During World War I, both British and German forces hid spies in plain sight. How? By digging up real bomb-blasted trees on battlefields during the night and replacing them with fake trees. The fake trees were hollow steel cylinders big enough for a soldier to hide in. Spies on both sides gathered intel that way for months with no one the wiser.

♥ DISGUISE #3: Sheep

♥ THE STORY: Two robbers who escaped from an Argentine prison in 2010 disguised themselves as sheep. When police came looking for them, they draped stolen sheep hides (complete with sheep heads) over themselves and mingled with real sheep in local flocks. The crooks evaded capture for more than a week, but...as one officer said, "They can't pull the wool over our eyes forever!"

Which disguise would you choose? _____

Why? _____

_____

Mastering Disguise

You have the CIA's entire disguise closet available to you, complete with masks, wigs, makeup, and everything else you might want to accomplish your mission. How would you disguise yourself in each of these situations?

YOUR MISSION: Investigate a "pig farmer" who is suspected of being an agent for S.P.A.M. (the Society for Pigs Against Mankind).
YOUR DISGUISE:

YOUR MISSION: Infiltrate a secretive magical society rumored to be planning to make the White House disappear.
YOUR DISGUISE:

YOUR MISSION: Search for alien artifacts in Roswell, New Mexico.
YOUR DISGUISE:

YOUR MISSION: Gather intel on a movie director who may be part of an international movie-pirating ring.

YOUR DISGUISE:

YOUR MISSION: Discover the soft-drink spy trying to steal the secret ingredients in Coca Cola.

YOUR DISGUISE:

YOUR MISSION: Find the pet store supplier who is smuggling exotic animals into the United States.

YOUR DISGUISE:

YOUR MISSION: Uncover the mastermind behind Nincompoops United, the notorious group of numbskulls bent on banning all books with the word "the" in them.

YOUR DISGUISE:

Draw Two!

My teacher gave us a worksheet about *homophones*, words that sound the same but mean different things. We're supposed to write examples, but I don't think she'll object to drawings, do you? Here's my first one. You can do the rest.

bored Kid

board Kid

eight books

ate books

bare legs

bear legs

scary ant

scary aunt

wild hair

wild hare

Free Fall!

Consider yourself warned! This is a trick question:

*If you were standing at the top of a tall
building and dropped a juice bottle and a grain
of rice at the same time, which would hit the
ground first? (Ignore air resistance.)*

The juice bottle, right? At least, that's what I thought.
Boy was I wrong. Turns out that in free fall, with no
air resistance, all dropped objects drop at the same rate.
That means the grain of rice and the bottle of juice
would hit the ground at the same time.

Why? Because without air resistance, gravity pulls
everything toward Earth's center at the same speed:
9.8 meters per second every second. (That's called "the
acceleration of gravity.") The acceleration of gravity
makes dropped objects speed up as they fall. The
faster an object is moving when it ENDS its fall, the
more energy and momentum it has. (Ever fallen off
something at the playground? The higher you are when
you start falling, the more it hurts when you hit the

ground.) Another way of thinking about it is that you weigh more upon impact when you fall from higher up. Don't believe me? Test it out. Stand on your bathroom scale and check your weigh. Then take a little jump and watch the number change when you land.

YOUR TURN! Drop things from different heights and record the results here. Do the things you drop bounce back up? Land with a thud? Take time to fall? *PS: If you drop anything that gets you in trouble, don't blame me!*

DATE:

What I Dropped:

What Happened:

DATE:

What I Dropped:

What Happened:

DATE:

What I Dropped:

What Happened:

DATE:

What I Dropped:

What Happened:

That's Super!

I think life as a superhero would be almost as awesome as life as a super-genius. First, you get to kick the bad guys' butts. You also you get to test out high-tech superhero gadgets and read the latest news about how super and heroic you are.

What could be tougher than being a superhero? Creating a superhero comic! Last weekend, I met a dynamic duo at a comics convention—Chris and Kyle Bolton. They're brothers who worked together to create *SMASH*, a comic novel about a 10-year-old superhero named Andrew Ryan. Chris writes the storylines and dialogue, and Kyle draws the pictures.

The brothers say making comics is super hard. Sometimes their stories stink at first, but they have to keep revising and revising until the stories are just right. "Failing again and again is the only way to succeed," Chris told me. "Finding out what doesn't work leads you to discover what does."

Create-a-Hero

List your superhero's powers:

What is your superhero's downfall?

Describe your superhero's super costume:

Who is your superhero's arch enemy?

DRAW YOUR SUPERHERO IN ACTION!

The WRITE Stuff

Yesterday, Ms. Kawolski told us Lola B.'s mom was coming for Career Day. She's a graphologist, so I was all ready to hear about graphs and other cool math-related things. Nope. Turns out *graphology* is the study of handwriting.

Lola's mom told the class that handwriting can reveal a lot about your personality. Companies hire her to do profiles of prospective employees. Police departments hire her to come up with personality profiles for crime suspects. (Just think! Someone could look at your handwriting and decide you're a criminal.)

Mrs. B. said cursive writing is easier to analyze than printing because it has more loops and swirls. But, she claimed, any writing sample can tell a graphologist at least a few things about you. Each of us got to write a paragraph for Lola's mom to analyze. She took one look at my handwriting and said, "You are a logical, practical person. You find it easy to focus on school work. But...sorry, dear...you're not very social."

Hmmmph! Some psychologists call graphology a *pseudoscience* (in other words, more fake than fact). Still, it might be useful for finding friends or watching out for frenemies. Here are a few notes I took on Career Day:

💚 If your handwriting slants to the right, you're probably a lot more social than I am.

💚 If your writing slants to the left, you might like to work behind the scenes instead of taking center stage.

💚 No slant? You're logical, practical, and not very social. (Guess that tells you which slant my writing has!)

💚 Are your letters giant? If so, you might have a "movie star" personality. If you write small, you're more likely to avoid the spotlight.

💚 Loopy letters? People who write with a lot of loops tend to be open-minded and spontaneous. If your loops are small or sharp, you're practical and set in your ways.

❦ Crossing your "t" with a long horizontal bar means you're very enthusiastic. If you cross your "t" above the stem, you're imaginative.

❦ If your handwriting slants up, you're creative and love life, kind of like Olivia the pig.

❦ If your handwriting slants down, you have an Eeyore outlook: you think things are bad and they're probably never going to get better.

❦ If you have an open loop in the letter "d" you probably take criticism too much to heart. If your "d" has a closed loop you probably don't.

❦ If the first hump in your "m" is taller, you are diplomatic and can communicate without hurting people's feelings. If the second hump is taller, you feel self-conscious if others criticize you.

Autograph Time!

Have fun with your signature! See if you can disguise it to bamboozle (confuse) a graphologist.

Sign your name as if you were....

... a 100-year-old grandmother:

... a supervillain:

... a foreign spy:

... a pop star:

... a toddler:

... the President:

... plotting to overthrow your school's principal:

You Rule the World

Actually, I plan to rule the world myself. But in case I don't succeed, give it your best shot! The last pages of *Uncle John's Do-It-Yourself Diary for Infomaniacs Only* are for you to record YOUR PLAN FOR WORLD DOMINATION.

HERE ARE THE RULES:

1. Include all the important things that happen in your life on the way to WORLD DOMINATION.

2. Draw comics to show how you went from being an INFOMANIACAL KID to RULER OF THE WORLD.

3. Add weird-but-true facts about whatever interests YOU.

4. HAVE FUN!!!!

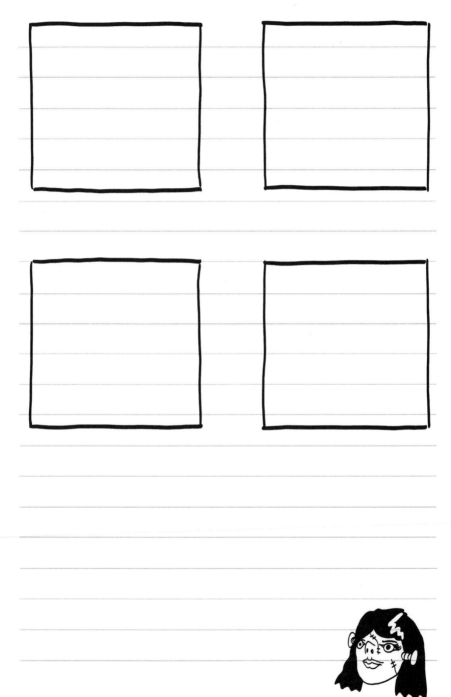

BRi Certificate of Completion

I _____ ,

[Name]

hereby certify that I completed
UNCLE JOHN'S D-I-Y DIARY
FOR INFOMANIACS ONLY

on _____ .

[date]

Tear out (or photocopy) this page and mail it to:
BRI, P.O. Box 1117, Ashland, Oregon 97520. You'll
receive a free BRI membership card, discounts
when ordering directly through the BRI, and a
permanent spot on the BRI honor roll!